I0606041

JASON BELONGS

For Rocky: Follow your music. Follow your heart. Love, Mom (A.A.)

To my Brother Adam with love, because you lent me your kippah. —J.S.M.

To my Little M, who filled me with love and creativity while working on every page of this lovely book. —I.M.

KAR-BEN PUBLISHING®
An imprint of Lerner Publishing Group, Inc.
241 First Avenue North
Minneapolis, MN 55401 USA
Website address: www.karben.com

Main body text set in ITC Franklin Gothic Std.
Typeface provided by Adobe Systems.

Library of Congress Cataloging-in-Publication Data

Names: Ades, Audrey, author. | McKinney, Jason Schachter, author. | Muñoz, Isabel, illustrator.
Title: Jason belongs / Audrey Ades and Jason Schachter McKinney ; illustrated by Isabel Muñoz.
Description: Minneapolis, MN : Kar-Ben Publishing, [2025] | Series: Jewish heroes | Audience: Ages 5–9 | Audience: Grades K–1 | Summary: "Jason loves to sing-until a whisper runs through school questioning whether Jason can be both Black and Jewish. Lifted up by both his African and Jewish ancestors' music, Jason finds a way to sing with his whole spirit"— Provided by publisher.
Identifiers: LCCN 2024037385 (print) | LCCN 2024037386 (ebook) | ISBN 9798765620809 (library binding) | ISBN 9798765675618 (epub)
Subjects: LCSH: McKinney, Jason Schachter—Juvenile literature. | African American cantors (Judaism)—Biography—Juvenile literature. | African American singers—Biography—Juvenile literature. | Jewish singers—United States—Biography—Juvenile literature. | African American Jews—Biography—Juvenile literature.
Classification: LCC ML3930.M385 A34 2025 (print) | LCC ML3930.M385 (ebook) | DDC 782.3/6092 [B]—dc23/eng/20241023

LC record available at https://lccn.loc.gov/2024037385
LC ebook record available at https://lccn.loc.gov/2024037386

Manufactured in Guang Dong, China by Dream Colour Printing
1-1011849-51830-11/25/2024

JASON BELONGS

THE STORY OF JASON SCHACHTER MCKINNEY

Audrey Ades *and* Jason Schachter McKinney

illustrated by Isabel Muñoz

KAR-BEN
PUBLISHING

Jason was proud of his family.
Daddy was a strong-spirited lawyer.
He believed that everyone had the right
to learn and love.

Mom was an artist and a teacher. She
had a heart as warm and soft as a loaf
of bread from Grandpa's bakery.

In Daddy's arms, Mom found a man who loved her as much as he loved justice. In Mom's arms, Daddy found comfort, happiness, and a religion that felt like home.

Mom and Daddy sent Jason to a Jewish day school where he learned Hebrew, Torah, and Jewish history.

Jason had his mom's heart, his daddy's spirit, and a sense of style that made people take notice.

Jason also had a BIG voice.

He sang in his school choir.

He sang prayers of hope
and thanksgiving.

And he rocked out on the playground.

Everybody liked Jason.

Or so it seemed.

One day, a cold, cruel whisper ran through school.

Jason is Black. Is he really Jewish?

How could they ask that? They'd been his classmates since first grade. They'd been to his home for Shabbat. They were at his bar mitzvah!

His rabbi said, “Don’t listen to them.”

His teachers said, “We love you, Jason.”

Jason loved being Jewish.
He loved his school.
But did he really belong?

The next year, Jason didn't go to a Jewish school.
His heart and spirit felt confused and sad.

He felt disconnected from his Jewish ancestors.

He stopped going to synagogue. He stopped caring about Jewish songs and prayers.

As Jason grew up, his voice sank down,

down,

down

into a beautiful baritone, deep and sweet as a river of honey.

He sang and acted in school plays,

he took voice lessons,

and he learned to play musical instruments.

Jason had a gift.

His voice belonged on the stage!

But Jason's gift for music needed more than his voice. For him to sing his best, his heart and spirit needed to feel happy. Accepted. Free.

Years earlier, his parents had taught him about Negro spirituals, songs of faith, hope, and thanks sung by the family's Black ancestors. The enslaved people who first sang these prayers dreamed that someday they would be free, accepted, and happy too.

Just when he needed it most, his African ancestors' music touched Jason's heart and spirit, lifting his voice to the heavens.

But Jason felt like an outsider when he prayed in an African American church. He hadn't been raised with this kind of worship, and it didn't come naturally to him.

He was Black. And he was Jewish.

Where did he belong?

When Jason sang on the stage, people smiled and clapped.

But that wasn't enough.

His heart and spirit still felt lonely and lost. He longed for a community where he could be everything he was—inside and out!

WHITE HOUSE
PRESERVATION HALL

Jason's singing career took him to concert halls around the world.

One Friday in Antwerp, Belgium, just around sunset, Jason was walking by a synagogue as Jews gathered to welcome the Sabbath. The golden light through the stained-glass windows gleamed like the Shabbat candles he remembered from home.

It had been many years since Jason had prayed in a synagogue. Was he ready to try again?

Jason sat down. In the last pew. Alone.

The cantor's voice floated from the bimah. Soulful. Joyous. Peaceful.

"Shalom Aleichem." *Peace to everyone*.

It had been a long time since Jason had heard that song.

The simple words echoed like a hug around his heart.

Jason began to sing.

A dozen faces turned around. A dozen welcoming smiles.

Jason smiled too.

Something sacred filled the room.

The next prayer began with the words "Tov l'hodot."

It is good to give thanks.

Jason gave thanks for his two beautiful cultures.

He was grateful to be an African American Jew.

He was grateful to be a Jewish African American.

After that night, Jason studied to become a cantor, a singer trained to lead Jewish congregations in prayer.

He prayed with congregations in synagogues around the world.

He sang songs from his African American heritage at churches and on stage.

He performed jazz at Preservation Hall, opera at the Lincoln Center, and Hanukkah songs at the White House.

And Jason belonged.

Everywhere.

ABOUT THE AUTHORS

AUDREY ADES is an author of picture books, including *Judah Touro Didn't Want to Be Famous, The Rabbi and the Reverend*, and *I Am Mozart, Too*. She lives in South Florida, where she has the best job in the world: writing about thoughtful, courageous people who make the world a better place. You can read more about her books at audreyadesbooks.com.

JASON SCHACHTER MCKINNEY is a music director, cantorial soloist, singer, composer, actor, conductor, and instrumentalist. His mixed heritage includes Native American, African American, European, and Jewish ancestry. He has written and composed original works for the theater titled *Moments with Paul* and *Frederick: A Musical Narrative*. He has performed these works about the great orators Paul Robeson and Frederick Douglass all over the world. McKinney lives in North Carolina with his wife, Karon.

ABOUT THE ILLUSTRATOR

ISABEL MUÑOZ is an illustrator of more than forty children's books. The Bright Agency has represented her since 2016. Previously, she studied fine arts at The Complutense University of Madrid. She grew up loving everything cute, spooky, and vintage, and drawing with her colored waxes (crayons) was her favorite childhood hobby. Isabel works from a lovely picture book-filled studio in magical Asturias, in northern Spain. She lives with her husband Fer, their baby Little M and their funny dog Pepi. You can follow her at www.isabelmg.com.